This book belongs to _____
created by God.

To Wanda, Ronald, Rodney, and Roderick,
the first children I ever loved

Large-quantity purchases or custom editions of this book are available at a discount from the publisher. For more information, contact the sales department at Augsburg Fortress, Publishers, 1-800-328-4648, or write to: Sales Director, Augsburg Fortress, Publishers, P.O. Box 1209, Minneapolis, MN 55440-1209.

Scripture passages are from the Contemporary English Version text, copyright © 1991, 1992, 1995 American Bible Society. Used by permission.

ISBN 0-8066-4553-9

The paper used in this publication meets the minimum requirements of American National Standard for Information Sciences—Permanence of Paper for Printed Library Materials, ANSI Z329.48-1984.

Manufactured in China

07   06   05   04   03   1   2   3   4   5   6   7   8   9   10

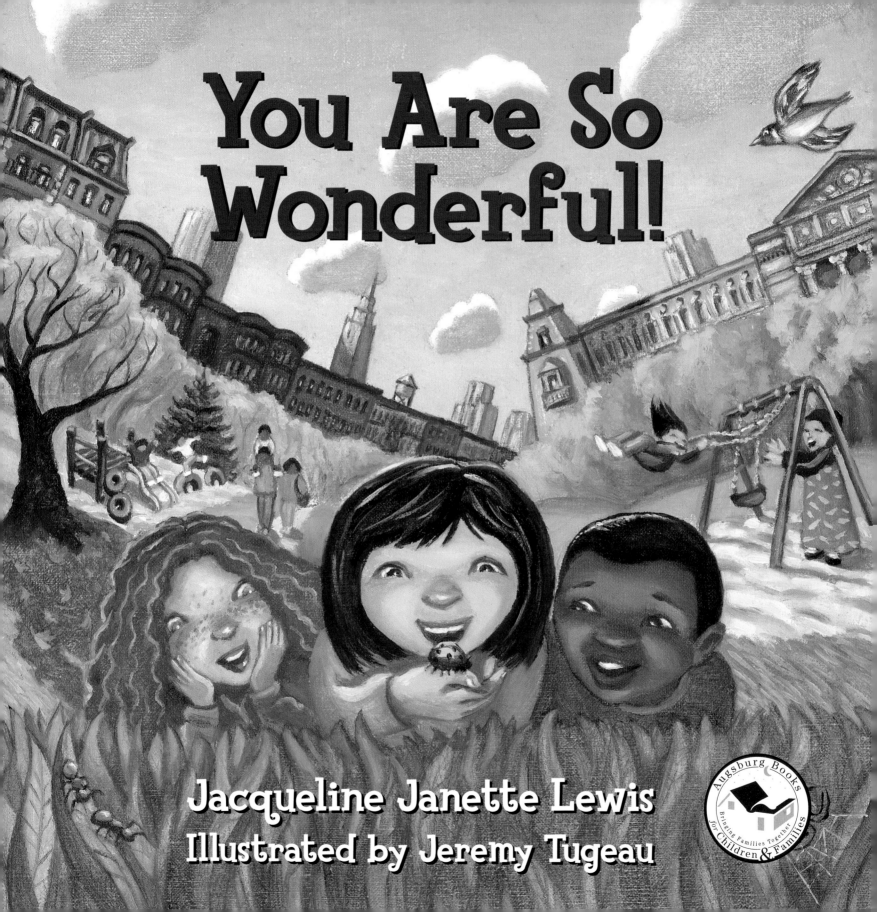

You Are So Wonderful!

Jacqueline Janette Lewis

Illustrated by Jeremy Tugeau

"You are the one who put
me together inside my
mother's body,

and I praise you because of the wonderful way you created me."
—Psalm 139:13

You are so wonderful. This is true.

God made no one else like you.

No one else has
a face like you.

No one else has feet like you.

No one else
has your nose.

No one else
has your toes.

No one else
has your grin.

No one else has your chin.

No one else has hands like these—

hands that help and make God pleased.

God made *you,*
made only one.

You are God's
daughter.

You are
God's son.

When we look the whole world through,

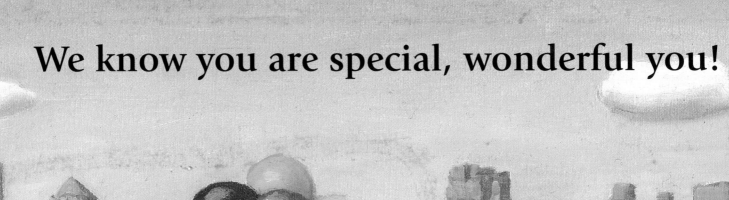

We know you are special, wonderful you!

"I praise you because of the wonderful way you created me." —Psalm 139:14a